THE CLARITY OF DISTANT THINGS

Jane Duran was born in Cuba and raised in the USA and Chile. Selections of her poems have appeared in *Poetry Introduction 8* (Faber 1993), *Making for Planet Alice* (Bloodaxe 1997), and *Modern Women Poets* (Bloodaxe 2005). In 1995 Enitharmon Press published her first full collection, *Breathe Now, Breathe* which won the Forward Prize for Best First Collection. Enitharmon also published four subsequent collections, including *Coastal* (2005) and *Graceline* (2010) which were both PBS Recommendations. Together with Gloria García Lorca, she translated Lorca's *Gypsy Ballads* (Enitharmon, 2011) and his *Sonnets of Dark Love* and *The Tamarit Divan* (Enitharmon, 2017). She received a Cholmondeley Award in 2005.

the clarity

of

distant things

JANE DURAN

CARCANET POETRY

First published in Great Britain in 2021 by
Carcanet
Alliance House, 30 Cross Street
Manchester, M2 7AQ
www.carcanet.co.uk

A CIP catalogue record for this book is
available from the British Library.

ISBN 978 1 80017 159 6

Book design by Andrew Latimer
Printed in Great Britain by SRP Ltd, Exeter, Devon

The publisher acknowledges financial
assistance from Arts Council England.

CONTENTS

gridlines

miniatures of Al-Andalus

for Gloria García Lorca

GRIDLINES

after Agnes Martin

When I first made a grid I happened to be thinking of the innocence of trees and then this grid came into my mind and I thought it represented innocence, and I still do, and so I painted it and then I was satisfied. I thought, this is my vision.

– Agnes Martin

THE TREE 1964
oil paint and graphite on canvas

inside the grid
I still recognise a tree

the tree occupies the grid
and is subsumed by it

unsettled also
in those wavering grid-lines

the grey oils
and graphite parallels

may also conceal the artist
in her studio

with her hair tied back
placing a wooden ladder

carefully by her canvas
so it holds steady

on the tilting floor
and she can climb

GRIDS OF INNOCENCE

in her grids of innocence
are grass or stone or morning

We'll know her spring field
by its fades and erasures

and starlight by its columns

How can we calibrate
the rose, when it is strafed

by intersecting lines
and an urban mist of skyscrapers

is blowing through
and around it?

BIG SKY

long before I could draw an even line
or stretch linen

over a wooden frame six foot square
stretch and stretch

the cloth taut, till my hands hurt

the big sky found me on the prairie
in Saskatchewan

where I could see far

and years later in desert country
it would still recognise me

across miles of flatland
staking out an enclosure in the wind

MACKLIN, SASKATCHEWAN, 1912

a settlement, her birthplace
a scattering of frame houses

here and here. Grain elevators
the Union Bank

a post office, pool room
two railway lines converge

the Empire Hotel , a harness shop

carriage tracks in the dirt
head off somewhere

a young woman on a doorstep
rubs her eyes

a dog on the road belongs to someone

WHEAT 1957
oil on canvas

I like to be here so far out
the wheat is this high

and now it is over my head
A farmhouse door opens wide

and a mother murmurs
oh where has she got to now?

alone in rustling air
bisecting a wheatfield

THE CLARITY OF DISTANT THINGS

today the wind is bringing me
a distant house, a barn

a train miles away
halted on the horizon

Each one, clarified
true in miniature

and with a glint
and outline of graphite

bears down on the prairie
Nowhere is far anymore

every remote narrative
makes its way forward

as the pure dry air
shrinks and engraves

AUTUMN PRAIRIE

the grasses on the prairie
go yellow, orange and brown

everywhere, till the ground
is what it might be like

in the end, ungrazed
beaten down, hymn-like

yet far from feeling
borne away to be born-again

for who can remember now
where even the palest green was

or what green thirsts for?

BLIZZARD

when the first snow flurries
passed our homestead

the low frame house
twelve by fourteen

and nearby stable
fourteen by sixteen

was it like my father
pulling on his boots

before dawn and opening
our door

to the prairie night

when I was only two
and so high, this high

but was it like my father dying
as the wind tried

to show the way along the road
until everywhere was road?

MILK RIVER 1963
oil and coloured pencil on linen

hear – from you,
hear, across

the wider
run of the river

where the current
is strongest

a word, a few words

COENTIES SLIP, NEW YORK, 1957–67

the old warehouses

gaze out to the East River
the Hudson River

and then beyond
as far as the estuary

and the Atlantic bay

Where am I now?
in a slipstream

in a bounteous air

where the streets give out
a rotating triangle

and my long stride

FRIENDSHIP 1963
incised gold leaf and gesso on canvas

in late afternoon
the rooftops elide

so many golden windows
bricks, dockside warehouses

artists' river-lofts
Over some the shine is fainter –

another light, another story –
but elsewhere it billows

like gold leaf over gesso
scored with a grid of rectangles

seizing all the light
it can capture at once

as those we adore do
who we want and trust

FALLING BLUE 1963
oil paint on canvas

now the riverbank can't see me
anymore, a distant warehouse –

smudges now
urgent, untroubled dusk

the blue and gold lines
are so closely packed

and uneven, they hum –
such night, such reckoning

ASSEMBLAGES, COENTIES SLIP

searching the docks
and demolition sites

I pick up discarded
boat spikes, wooden pegs

bottle caps, knobs
steel bolts with rotted heads

stencils, brass brad nails
silver wire, nights

and the scavenging
wind from the river

WATER 1958
painted wire and bottle caps mounted on wood

batten down the water
with bottle caps

or those painted wires
will blow away –

when you line them up
keep the wires taut

and confined
in their deep currents

the wind here is dangerous
immerse yourself

THE LAWS 1958
boat spikes and oil paint on wood

how embedded they are
aligned, row after row

how they pierce and rust
and fasten

while the lower half
of the grey wood

is bare
lawless and riven

LITTLE SISTER 1962

oil paint, ink and brass nails on canvas and wood

a dotted interior grid
on khaki oil paint

braced, buttressed
with brass nails

each placed just so
the skittering black

ink lines, small
buttons on your dress

we go where we go

HORIZON 1960
oil paint on canvas

the repetitive horizons tremble

rows of blue-grey triangles
– or are they mountains?

rest on loosely parallel
horizontal lines

just before daybreak
or nightfall

Each mountain has its own
hint of light

on the summit
down the edge of a slope

or along the base
Is somewhere home?

WHITE FLOWER 1960
oil paint on canvas
     for Stephen Stuart-Smith

I have to search for it
comb the air for it

the sleep it engenders in brown
soil it coincides with

coincidental pressures which
deepen or raise it

into every moment of light
allowed it

by a picket fence, a harbour
or bent down by the wind

on a hill
all the magnetised white inscriptions

SUMMER 1964

watercolour, ink and gouache on paper

already gone – summer
wearing out the trees

the clouds marooned, serene
or travelling in haste – were they?

a deeper blue in the top
right hand corner of the sky

and the mountains –
were they invited to watch how

one cloud imitated the gesture
of a tree looking the other way

in the wind
with a certain authority?

THE PEACH 1964
graphite and ink on paper mounted on board

well, it's forgotten now
that peach I knew

I bit into
that gave me back

only beige, graphite,
ink, sanity

and orchard after orchard

GRID

some days I also search
for its certainty

with tape or string
a T-square, pencil

or paint. I lean into it

here and there a tremor
in my hand indicates

a slight give, a looseness
or elasticity

THE TREE 1964
oil paint and graphite on canvas

I must visit my tree
one last time

so I will have no regrets

before it disperses entirely
before it disappears

into the wind
of grey rectangles

THE SCOURING

how will it end

the way the wind
loosens things

scours, scores
and abandons?

After the electroshock
therapy at Bellevue

and she takes off
in a white pickup truck

old landmarks
vanish

her eyes squinting
in the sunlight

her downcast eyes
her bewildered eyes

ROAD TRIP 1967–68

The solitary life is full of terrors… – Agnes Martin

ah the dust I kick up
disturbing the landscape

when I turn my pickup
in a blur of desert

Here is country I recognise
a rejection, flatland

and the innocent
pastimes of air

whenever I stop
and roll down

my window
key in the ignition

spoon in a tin cup

PORTALES MESA, NEW MEXICO, 1968–77

any arrival is a warning, the limpid air
a mask, or a deep wall

through which a friend, artist
or admirer has to travel

to get to her
The road does not know the way

and fails to see her
in her campervan where she lives

on Knox gelatin, orange juice
and bananas

ONE-ROOM ADOBE

I smooth a layer of mud
over the adobe walls

although the grid made
by the adjoining bricks

still burns through
Nothing is missing here

the high mesa rolls out
pine trees for a log studio

dirt, straw and pine
are here for the taking

sagebrush flats, dry riverbed
no one to talk to

ON A CLEAR DAY 1973
portfolio of 30 screenprints

a coolness can enter the page
open endearments in grey ink

a light touch restores
all that is present of peace

a rejoicing grid
has been there all along

under everything I see
wherever I am

wherever I happen to be

UNTITLED 1977
watercolour and graphite on paper

the paper rucks
wrinkling the watercolour

and bands of diluted blue
peach and white

vanish
Which house did I enter

which summer will remember me?
It betrays no story or place

but a mood, an intention
This one! I stop before it

and find myself, a child still
too dazzled to bear these pallors

GALISTEO, NEW MEXICO, 1978

wherever grid lines
intersect, they linger

a moment together
as if to draw breath

then continue
setting out for somewhere

faraway and envisaged
but here between Highway 41

and Galisteo Creek
I cover my campervan

with adobe
there are openings in the walls

to coincide
with the camper windows

so light can still enter
and the land

THE SABLE BRUSH

by now the light is going,
run to ground

but all day nothing impedes it
everywhere is open space

sunlight prepares me
the way I prime my canvas

with gesso and lay acrylic blues
vertically along horizontal bands

with a new red sable brush
one inch wide

FARAWAY LOVE 1999
acrylic and graphite on canvas

most elusive
is where the blue

almost turns white

I've seen you now
It's alright. I keep leaving

and finding you here again

turning my car
into the same old town

among strangers

NIGHT SEA 1963
oil and gold leaf on canvas

a furtive night sea moves under
and over a grid of 2976 rectangles –
a worn, illusory net, gilded

surfacing and reassuring
with tiny flaws and deformations
you only see if you are close up

Through the ultramarine you can glimpse
reflections rising from a thin
white ground made of titanium

lead and zinc pigments, and below
the taut linen holds the sea-drift in place
But if you stand far back

the grid disappears (like the occasional
paintbrush hairs caught in the oils)
and there is our night sea, opaque

RED BIRD 1964
acrylic and coloured pencil on canvas

almost I can't see it
I can't see

where it happens
the locality is unsettling

a road? A noon road?
A tree I keep passing?

Red pencil lines
so faint, so close together

they merge and bind
and staunch

A life the wind catches at?
Oh one!

MINIATURES OF AL-ANDALUS

CROSSING TO HISPANIA, 711

to conjure the hour of departure

press Tariq ibn Ziyad, his soldiers
horses, spears and banners

close together on ships tossing
cheerfully side by side

and scale them down many times

Paint the illuminated wind
the open strait, small and confined

as if held in the palm of a child's hand

Erase all terror, hope or ambition –
each one vast and morbid –

from the faces of the soldiers
so they are stern and eager to a man

ready for the night crossing ahead
and a candle flame of land

RAIDS

who here can read
the script of their arrival

cursive and troubling?
Any one of them

riding past our farms
may lean down

and cut a deep line of blood
through the earth

and it will heal

TO PAINT THE CLAMOUR

even seven horsemen will do

riding elbow to elbow
beard to beard

so they seem more –
an army of multitudes

the uplifted faces and long
gold trumpets

the deep drums
and hooves, the hooves

all suddenly near

as the wind circling your house
as your own quiet and diligence

THE SPOILS

did the soldiers gather
and drive the baleful sheep

cows and goats
before them, trampling

the meadow flowers?
And did the elderly olive trees

shiver on hillocks
and the grasses stand on end?

CÓRDOBA

all the prismatic illusion
Jew Christian Muslim

gardens and inner courtyards
inner, the inner man

striding or stumbling into light
and radial encounters

in streets and marketplaces
a glance, a warm greeting

JOURNEYS

red and white fish
nose the hull

an old man is at the tiller
and a child tightens the sail

He glances at the black calligraphy
in the sky and three travellers

in gold and blue turbans
are deep in consultation

on important matters –
sometimes their turbans even touch

THE LIBRARY

Let Scripture be your Eden,
and the Arabs' books your paradise grove...
Dunash Ben Labrat

seven men sit close together on cushions
so their blue and red robes overlap

One holds an open book
On the shelves above them, laid flat

are astronomical charts, philosophical
manuscripts, treatises on medicine

theology, music and agriculture
In such surroundings the mind darts

to bold or extravagant conclusions
and robust and earnest questions

ALIF

alif, the first vertical
stroke
in the alphabet

against which
the other letters
may be calibrated

Even the sun
and seasons
spiral

and question
this perfectly
intentional axis

MENORAH

a little rain, longed for
a struggle

in the spiritual heat
The door of a synagogue

opens briefly
oh you have captured me

menorah
The night is serious

the night is scholarly
with seven flames

MADINAT AL-ZAHRA

for Bachira Taouti

below the palace
the Guadalquivir valley

sweeps away in the sun
and wind

sweeps and is held
still and immersed

and may seem gilded
or illusory

to the one who praises

PAINTED BOWL FROM MEDINA ELVIRA

a green horse rises up
piecemeal and sturdy

his black mane falling in damp
strands down his neck

the seal of his round hooves
on the hot, dry earth of Madinat Ilbira

Two fragments join his knotted tail

A bird balances on the saddle
one wing raised, the other lowered

It holds the reins in its beak
but those reins are a mere thread

looped casually over three breakages

How did the artist imagine
that an affinity might unite

bird and horse, might allow
a bird to guide a horse simply

by holding a thread in its beak?

The artist in his room
the horse in his bowl

the archaeologist in his dig
an elated bird alighting on each

from who knows where

BRONZE PERFUME BOTTLE, CÓRDOBA

the loops of cord
and teardrop motifs

in relief
round its body

the garland of acanthus
and the encircling

horseshoe arches
with trifoliate leaves

a chained stopper
scored with radii

and enclosure, I think of enclosure

WATER CLOCK

Al-Zarqali's water clocks
were two marble basins
housed on the outskirts of Toledo

by the banks of the River Tajo
and connected to it
by underground conduits

As the moon waxed
each day the basins filled
with half a seventh part

of water, and as it waned
each day they emptied
by half a seventh part

so by the fourteenth day
the basins were brimful
and by the end of the month

not a drop remained
thus mapping the hours
and a lunar calendar

Water preoccupied
with time and time alone
as it continued to flow –

true, pure, cold time
liquid, embodied
well into the next century

when King Alfonso VII
ordered one of the clocks
to be dismantled

He wished to discover
its inner workings
and practical mysteries

so in the year 528 of the Hegira
the astronomer Hamis ibn Zabara
took the clock apart

hoping to study and perfect
its mechanism
but neither he nor anyone else

was able to reassemble it
after such a consummate
and precise dismantling

RAISINS

Kitab al-Filaha* by Abu 'l-Khayr

gather the ripe grapes at midday
and spread them on level sand

until they shrivel and redden a little
and fall away if you touch them

then leave them to the night dew

and in the early morning
carry the clusters home to bind

in woven halfa and hang
from nails in walls and beams

only parts of his manuscript
are preserved in Paris, Rabat

and Tetouan, the lost folios
scattered where, by whose touch?

We know so little about him

but I imagine his home in Sevilla
the cool and darkness there

in the early morning
as he hurries in with the raisins

the dew he brings in

---
* *Book of Agriculture*

THE GARDENS
*Kitab al-Filaha** by Ibn al-Awwam

Ibn al-Awwam advises
shading wells

and pools with trees –
he suggests poplars

wild pomegranates
willows, elms

azedarachs
and mountain ashes

You can even hang
trellises of vines

from the tall trees
as ornaments

The water below
will stay cool for irrigation

His farmland in Aljarafe
his face in the shade

the planting and possession
of shade over water

---

* *Book of Agriculture*

BRASS ASTROLABE
for Redha

to read brevity
you need patient

meticulous time

a holding plate –
its raised circumference

scored with hours
and 360 degrees –

to store 5 discs of the earth
the sheen of 5 latitudes

5 meridians
and local horizons

earth you can touch
your forehead to, your lips to

and a perforated disc
that rotates

with a carved ecliptic
and 23 brass pointers

(the silver studs missing now)
for 24 stars

migrating overhead
their names engraved

in Kufic script
for the language-gazers

TABULA ROGERIANA

The earth is round like a sphere, and the waters adhere to it...
Muhammad al-Idrisi

the earth wants something of us
It surpasses our meagreness

basking upside down
in al-Idrisi's map –

south is at the top
so the right-hand corner

of north Africa reaches down
to touch al-Andalus

which reaches warmly up
The yellowing lands

and diluted blues spread
beyond their geographical

coordinates across Eurasia
in that enquiring, calm

way that maps have
no wind, no din

HADITH BAYAD WA RIYAD

I did not sleep to rest but in the hope that my beloved would appear.

Riyad

so much has worn away
I can just make out
the alarmed gestures of women
how many? in an alcove

bending over her to sprinkle
camphor and rose water
A woman has fainted
her face is featureless

but the folds of her robe
are a dark, sure green
whereas the refined palace
architecture is left to us

in all its detail, the two towers
linked by a row of horseshoe arches
and window grilles
with indented lozenge patterns

Each tower has a peaked roof
(one orange, one green)
with eight slopes for eight
waters to slide down

but inside the palace
those nearly effaced women
are only traces now
eyebrows, part of a cloak

a pink sleeve, two arms raised
yet through their tumult
a few glints of gold leaf
come to rescue us here

Bayad

a young man in love
lies on blades of grass
without crushing them

one arm outstretched
his turban unravelling
His hand, too, is expressive

delicate, draped over the water
where vertical black
and green river lines

pursue each other
Two cypresses are dense
with a pungent inner life

An inky waterwheel
is in the foreground
but it is small as if it were

actually in the distance
lifting and dripping water
as it rotates and creaks

OIL LAMP
for Cheli

of all, this one
is the one I long to see by

plain, rough
with a long runnel

for the soaking wick
and the run of flame

it's just there
where the oil burned

night after night
it's that scorch mark

I can't turn away from
or see beyond

IN THE *CANTIGAS*

between thumb and forefinger
our days are thin

and tortuous grey waves
curl as far as the castle door

A fishing net
is cast out over the waters

A pensive lute player
in a red robe

edges one foot over
the edge of the frame

MINIATURE OF ALFONSO X THE WISE ON HORSEBACK

from the monastic cartulary, Santiago de Compostela, thirteenth century

his horse is also fabular –
the pale blue polka-dot legs and belly

a castle painted on its red-ochre neck
Grey lions rear up on a white

and gold blanket thrown over
the generous back and haunches

Against a grid of tiny squares in royal
blue or fading, the rider holds a lance –

its point runs through the border
His shield repeats the lions and castle

He leans a little forward in the saddle
with what certainty! His crown tilts

King of all Castilla and León
how calm he is, how lithe and agile

even in battle he is measured and equable
His soft boots curl over his stirrups

CANTIGA 181: THE BANNER OF THE VIRGIN DEFEATS THE MOORS AT MARRAKESH

look at the horses, multiple profiles
dense albums of legs

When two armies face each other

they jostle in the smallest of spaces
barely able to move

so intricately engaged are they
in giving and receiving blows

The retreating soldiers
ride facing backwards

holding up their shields

What are they riding towards?

A tree, a river torrent
a vaulting mountain

the warm touch of a hand

THE MIRACLES OF SANTA MARÍA

a runaway calf
finds his way into a church

and devout silkworms
spin two veils

for the Virgin
who can and does heal

a leper's body
with milk from her breast

In Orleans her statue
raises one knee

to intercept an arrow
(the arrow is still embedded

there, the knee still raised)
and she stands

on a ship's masthead
during a terrifying storm

White bees rush
through a hole

in a church wall
to repair the half-melted

Paschal candle
and a monk in a garden

listens to birdsong
for 300 years

SIEGE

each castle turret
hides another

and bearded soldiers fall
head first

from the parapets
down to the scorched grass

and long-stemmed
red and blue flowers

CHESS GAME

two men, a Christian and a Muslim,
sit on red and black striped cushions

a chessboard between them
The tent is inscribed with a line

of blue calligraphy
The bearded man in a white turban

may be losing and holds up one hand
but the game is amicable

the thin bareheaded young man
relaxed and conciliatory

The two men gaze now and then
out at a billowing landscape

Whose pawns are deaf to entreaties
whose freedom and impulses

are reined in?
Whose knight will know a harsher meadow

where dire battles gleam?
But for now all four knights can leap

over orchards, rivers, mountains
and there is always a last chance, castling

THE POWERFUL

in the room of the powerful and wise
some have hennaed beards

their long hands converse with each other
and they look away, explaining

Whereas, whereas they say
or Who will prevail?

The earth is turning crimson
on battlefields

yet the sky we lean back against
is still beaten gold

CERAMICS
for Mimi Khalvati

stay, a little while
with me

pale green horse
from Medina Elvira

stay, two Nasrid
wading birds

facing each other
under a myrtle tree

NASRID LUSTREWARE

a gold brown ship
spins in the sun

sails, bow and stern curve
up the walls of the bowl

to a fine cobalt rim
no one is going anywhere

four fish swim underneath
in the glare

the ship tosses
in the noon of its enquiry

RECONQUEST

it falls to each soldier

to be wide-eyed and resolute
in the stillness

the peace of a miniature

where the clash
of shield and sword

horse and sky
is always harmonious

and exacting, silently endured

CARAVEL

socarrat tile from Paterna

how passionate, prow
and stern

almost touch
the red-ochre stars

and palmate suns

Even the sharks leap up
devotional

from the scorched
wavy lines

sea water makes

The reeling masts
crow's nest

and sunshade sail
all reach up, up

to those outbursts
in the night sky

as a memory
or an invocation

WHEN THEY LEFT, 1492

if I were a seller of candles,
        the sun would never go down
    Avraham ibn Ezra

when they left, however they left
they went wide

I'm listening now not to their voices
a turbulence

but to a key closing up a house

If I look it is not to meet his eyes
but to see him in his doorway

as if he were entering

BAPTISM OF MUSLIM WOMEN

wooden bas-relief by Felipe Bigarny, Capilla Real, Granada, 1522

one of the friars carries a processional
cross, and with his free hand

he raises the veil of a woman
to baptise her

There is a hefty, ornate font
where wooden water swirls – a centripetal

and also a centrifugal force
More than forty women

overlap each other, elevated
in rows up the carved panel

Why so many at once?
Are there more beyond?

No one can move suddenly away
in the robust circumstances of wood

MORISCOS

after an anonymous seventeenth-century painting

why is the harbour crowded
with departing boats

and the shore with horsemen
and covered wagons?

Who are the people walking in single file
down the mountain to the water?

Are they moving steadily
or is the mountain delaying them

like a child clinging to his father's legs?
Who is the tall man in black

at the portside, with a red cross
sewn on his doublet?

Why is the sky turning dark over Vinaroz
why is the sea so final?

AMONG THE CLARITIES

what happens to perception
when the night
reclaims what is scattered?

*

even church bells can throw stones
and the early morning wind
goad you

*

I dig my fingers into the rind
of an orange
but the fruit is powdery

*

the sacked libraries
burned books

the fiery river –
a girl recklessly

places one drop from it
behind each ear

*

the voice of a muezzin
churchbells
or the Shema

each has its own
quiet afterwards

*

along the riverbank
the turning waterwheels
are glorious

the valley lucent

*

a leather binding of a Quran
may be a door

a central, eight-pointed star
strapwork and gold leaf

so much to preoccupy the eye
and breath

*

stout breezes by the Guadiana
and the Guadalquivir

a last refuge in the Alpujarras
night, its lanterns and listeners

      *

a fish struggles through turquoise
spiral waves, surges

a coastline, then no coastline
wind, then no wind
blue smoke, carrion

      *

whether the cry of a baby
or the cries of seagulls
both tear the air

      *

Riyad takes the *oud* in her arms
and sings

among the clarities
each illumination
is too close to bear

RED EARTH

in my hands I take that red earth
that crops up everywhere

crumbles and clings
I see it here and there

in vineyards
or running with the urine of horses

on dirt roads
its light is in the red tiles

on the roofs of long farms
and in the clay terrain

of ceramic bowls and oil lamps
It is the idea of staying, a grant of earth

the earth I interrupt now with my hands

GRIDLINES

This sequence was first inspired and informed by visits to the
Agnes Martin exhibition at the Tate Modern in 2015, and
the exhibition catalogue: *Agnes Martin,* Tate Publishing 2015.
Among the books I have consulted in researching the work
and life of Agnes Martin, particularly illuminating for me was
the comprehensive and insightful: *Agnes Martin: Her Life and
Art* by Nancy Princenthal, Thames and Hudson 2015.

'Macklin, Saskattchewan, 1912' and 'blizzard'
Agnes Martin was born in 1912 in Macklin on the
Saskatchewan prairie. Her family were among the early
homesteaders and her father was a wheat farmer. After he died
in 1914 the family moved away to Lumsden, although there
is some evidence that they also continued to spend time in
Macklin until 1916.

'the clarity of distant things'
This title is a quote from a talk given for the Tate by Nancy
Princenthal on Agnes Martin in 2015, entitled *Innocence the
Hard Way*. During the talk she referred to Agnes Martin's
early watercolour *New Mexico Mountain Landscape, Taos* and
said of the painting 'I think it does give you the sense of the
clarity of distant things in the New Mexico landscape'.

'Coenties Slip, New York, 1957–67'
In 1931 Agnes Martin followed her sister to the USA,
In the 1940s she studied Fine Arts and Arts Education at
the Teachers College, Columbia University, and art at the
University of Mexico in Albuquerque and Taos. Her earliest
surviving works were painted in New Mexico.

In 1957 she moved to Coenties Slip on the wharves of lower Manhattan, among a group of artists including Jasper Johns, Ellsworth Kelly and Robert Rauschenberg. Her exploration of the grid in her paintings dates from this period. Her work was exhibited at a number of galleries and museums, including the Betty Parsons Gallery and the Robert Elkon Gallery.

'Assemblages'
During her time at Coenties Slip she began to work with local materials scavenged from docks and building sites to create assemblages.

'the scouring' and 'road trip 1967–68'
Agnes Martin suffered schizophrenic episodes and at Bellevue Hospital she received electric shock treatment. In 1967 she abandoned Coenties Slip and set off in a pickup truck for a solitary journey in the US west and Canada.

'Portales mesa, New Mexico, 1968–77' and 'Galisteo, New Mexico, 1978'
Martin finally settled in New Mexico in 1968, first on the Portales mesa near Cuba where she began to paint again, and then in Galisteo from 1978. In the early nineties her work was shown in solo exhibitions in European cities. She moved to Taos New Mexico in 1993 where she lived and painted until her death in 2004.

'*Night Sea* 1963'
This poem draws on the technical analysis of the painting in Suzanne Hudson's *Night Sea*, Afterall Books, 2016; and in Christina Bryan Rosenberger's essay 'A Sophisticated Economy of Means: Agnes Martin's Materiality' in *Agnes Martin* (Dia Art Foundation and Yale University Press, 2014).

The poems are glimpses of the long period of Muslim rule in Iberia and its immediate aftermath, from the first Berber and Arab invasion in 711, through to the Christian reconquest of the last stronghold of Granada and the subsequent expulsion of Jews and Muslims from the Peninsula. The Arabic name given to the Iberian territories under Islamic rule was *al-Andalus*.

In the chronology of the seven centuries of Islamic rule, in broad brushstrokes and with approximate dates a number of phases can be highlighted: a period of Umayyad rule from Córdoba, initially by governors, then Emirs and finally Caliphs (711–1031); following civil war, the replacement of the Umayyad caliphate by small *Taifa* kingdoms (1031–1086); a period of Almoravid, followed by Almohad, rule (1088–1232), both maintaining central power in Marrakesh, with Sevilla becoming the Almohad capital; and the Nasrid Kingdom (1238–1492) with its capital in Granada.

Whereas by 1031 most of the Peninsula (including what is now Portugal) was under Islamic rule, over the centuries internal discord and successive battles with Christian Iberia resulted in the erosion of al-Andalus, until finally only the Nasrid kingdom of Granada remained. During the seven centuries of al-Andalus, an extraordinary, diverse cultural life and scholarship developed, in which the arts and sciences flourished. For many reasons, war and religious purges among them, large numbers of Arabic documents and manuscripts, miniatures included, were lost.

A number of the poems in this sequence are inspired by art and artefacts from the time of al-Andalus, including illuminated miniatures from the thirteenth-century *Cantigas de Santa María* commissioned by King Alfonso X. The *Cantigas* comprise 420 poems written in Galician-Portuguese, praising, and narrating the miracles of the Virgin Mary. In all but one of the surviving four manuscripts, each poem is accompanied by musical notation. In two of the manuscripts, the poems are illustrated by miniatures, in themselves revealing of many aspects of life during al-Andalus.

Jesús Greus' *Así Vivieron en al-Andalus* (Grupo Anaya S.A. 2013) offered a helpful introduction to the subject. As the scope of my sequence widened, among the books I consulted, crucial in my research was *Al-Andalus: The Art of Islamic Spain* published by the Metropolitan Museum of Art, New York in 1992, which provides detailed information on some of the artefacts evoked in the poems.

'Córdoba'
Co-existence with and tolerance of the Christian and Jewish religions was a characteristic of Muslim governance in al-Andalus and markedly so in Córdoba under Umayyad rule. Though Christans and Jews did not have equal status and certain restrictions were imposed on them in Muslim Iberia, they could practice their religions and were protected under the Quranic dispensation accorded to 'People of the Book', and were able to contribute to and participate in a rich cultural and intellectual landscape. This tolerance and *convivencia* had its later exceptions, particularly under the more austere Almohad rule.

'Madinat al-Zahra'
This palace city was built in the tenth century by Abd al-Rahman III on the slopes of the Sierra Morena, overlooking the Guadalquivir Valley.

'journeys' and 'the library'
These poems drew on two miniatures in al-Hariri's *Maqamat* painted by al-Wasiti in thirteenth-century Iraq. Libraries

proliferated in Muslim Iberia. The library of Córdoba, first established under Abd al-Rahman II, by the tenth century under al-Hakam II is said to have housed some 400,000 books. The epigraph in the library, a fragment by tenth-century Hebrew poet Dunash Ben Labrat, was translated by Peter Cole in his book *The Dream of the Poem*: Hebrew Poetry from Muslim and Christian Spain 950–1492.

'painted bowl from Medina Elvira'
Fragments of this 10th century bowl were discovered during excavations on the site of Madinat Ilbira (now Medina Elvira), Granada. Pieced together, the bowl is now in the Museo Arqueológico de Granada.

'bronze perfume bottle'
this tenth-century bottle is from Olivos Borrachos and is now in the Museo Arqueológico de Granada.

'brass astrolabe'
'The astrolabe was transmitted to Europe mainly by way of al-Andalus and became the most popular European instrument during the Middle Ages and the Renaissance.' (Al-Andalus: The Art of Islamic Spain, The Metropolitan Museum of Art, 1992).

The astrolabe described in the poem was made by Ahmad ibn Muhammad al-Naqqash, Zaragoza, and dated 1079-80.

'water clock'
Abu Ishaq Ibrahim ibn Yahya al-Naqqash al-Zarqali (1029–1087) was an inventor and astronomer. He fled Toledo when the city was under attack by Alfonso VI, the Christian King of Castilla. The poem is informed by the account of al-Zarqali's water clocks by Mohammed ibn Abi Bakr al-Zuhri, a geographer from Granada.

'raisins'

The agronomist and botanist Abu 'l-Khayr al-Ishbili was a contemporary of King al-Mu'tamid who reigned in Sevilla from 1069 to 1091. He was admired by Ibn al-Awwam who cited him in his own *Kitab al-Filaha*, including in his chapter on gardens. The italicised instructions on the cultivation of raisins drawn from 'l-Khayr's book (of which there is no extant complete copy), have been condensed in the poem.

'the gardens'

Abu Zakariya ibn al-Awwam's extensive and miraculously preserved treatise on agriculture, *Kitab al-Filaha*, is a compilation of advice and practice of Byzantine and Middle Eastern Arabic agronomists, as well as those from al-Andalus, while also drawing on his own experience as a farmer. Apart from what can be gleaned from his book, little is known of his life. He lived in Sevilla in the second part of the twelfth century and perhaps the beginning of the thirteenth century.

'Tabula Rogeriana'

The geographer Abu 'Abd Allah Muhammad al-Idrisi was born around 1100 in Sabta (present-day Ceuta in Morocco). He studied in Córdoba and travelled extensively in southern regions of the Iberian peninsula, North Africa and as far as Damascus. King Roger II of Sicily invited him to his court (around 1138) and commissioned al-Idrisi's renowned book on geography which includes a detailed world map and extensive commentaries.

'Hadith Bayad wa Riyad'

The only surviving miniatures from al-Andalus itself that have come to light are from the *Hadith Bayad wa Riyad*, a love story probably written during the period of the Almohad dominion. Although purges by both Christians and Muslims meant that many thousands of valuable manuscripts were destroyed or lost, the beauty and refinement of the miniatures illustrating this story suggest that this form of art was widely practiced and developed in al-Andalus.

'miniature of Alfonso X the Wise on Horseback'
Alfonso X reigned from 1252 until his death in 1284. At the time of his reign the Almohads had been defeated and most of Spain had been reclaimed by Christian monarchs, though al-Andalus held on in southern Spain as principalities and the Nasrid kingdom. Alfonso X was known as *El Sabio* (the Wise): he fostered learning and scholarship, including the extensive translation of Arabic and Latin texts into Castilian.

'chess game'
This poem is inspired by a miniature from Alfonso X's *Libro de Juegos* (Book of Games) completed in 1283.

'the powerful'
This poem is after a mural in the *Sala de los Reyes* in the Alhambra, Granada.

'Nasrid lustreware'
This bowl was made in Málaga between 1425 and 1450 and is now in the Victoria and Albert Museum.

'caravel'
Socarrat tiles were made by *mudéjar* artisans. The term *mudéjar* refers to Muslims living in Christian territories. This *socarrat* is from fourteenth-century Paterna in Valencia, then under Christian domination. The word *socarrat* means 'scorched'.

'when they left'
Following the fall of Granada and the brutal persecution by the Inquisition of *conversos* (converts to Christianity) suspected of practising the Jewish faith, the Catholic monarchs Fernando and Isabel issued a Charter of Expulsion. In this Charter, all Jews refusing to convert to Christianity were ordered to leave the country. Between 100,000 and 150,000 Jews went into exile in 1492. The epigraph is from a poem by Avraham Ibn Ezra (c.1093–c.1167) translated by Peter Cole in his book *The Dream of the Poem*.

'baptism of Muslim women'
after the recapture of Granada by the Catholic monarchs Fernando and Isabel, tolerance and freedom of worship was promised in the *Capitulations of Granada*. However this was followed by mass forced baptisms of Muslims and the burning of thousands of Arabic books in Granada.

'moriscos'
the *moriscos* were the Muslims and their descendants who were forced to convert to Christianity following the fall of Granada in 1492. In 1609, an edict issued by King Felipe ordered the expulsion of all *moriscos* from Spain.

ACKNOWLEDGMENTS

Moniza Alvi read my manuscript as it evolved through various stages and her detailed and perceptive comments have been wonderfully helpful and inspiriting. My warm thanks to Mimi Khalvati for her close reading of the manuscript and for her valuable insights and advice. I am grateful to Gloria García Lorca and Stephen Stuart-Smith for their feedback on the manuscript at early stages, and to Nancy Mattson for her thoughful comments on *gridlines*. My sister Cheli Durán's suggestion that I write about al-Andalus first sparked the sequence. My warm thanks to Bachira Taouti for her translations of some Arabic texts.

A version of the poem '*The Tree*, 1964' was published in *Travelling Ladders* (The Poetry Trust, 2015). A number of these poems were published in *PN Review*.

I am immensely grateful to Michael Schmidt for publishing this book, to John McAuliffe for his sensitive editorial advice and to Andrew Latimer for his patient collaboration and beautiful cover design.

Special thanks are due to Stephen Stuart-Smith, and to Wendy Brandmark, Michele Sigler and the poets in my Thursday Group for their support and abiding friendship. My heartfelt thanks to my husband Redha and son Ramy for all their support and encouragement.